D0442587

His Princess Bride

His Princess Bride

Love Letters from Your Prince

Sheri Rose SHEPHERD

Revell

a division of Baker Publishing Group
Grand Rapids, Michigan

© 2008 by Sheri Rose Shepherd

Published by Revell
a division of Baker Publishing Group
P.O. Box 6287, Grand Rapids, MI 49516-6287
www.revellbooks.com

Printed in Singapore by KHL Printing Co. Pte Ltd

ISBN 978-0-8007-1915-9

Scripture

Unless otherwise indicated, Scripture is taken from the *Holy Bible*, New Living
Translation, copyright © 1996. Used by permission of Tyndale House Publishers,
Inc., Wheaton, Illinois 60189. All rights reserved.

Scripture marked CEV is taken from the Contemporary English Version © 1991,
1992, 1995 by American Bible Society. Used by permission.

Scripture marked NIV is taken from the HOLY BIBLE, NEW INTERNATIONAL
VERSION®. NIV®. Copyright © 1973, 1978, 1984 by International Bible Society.
Used by permission of Zondervan. All rights reserved.

His Princess ® is a registered trademark of Sheri Rose Shepherd and His Princess
Ministries.

Contents

ACKNOWLEDGMENTS

This book would not be possible if not for the love and support of my husband, Steven Gene Shepherd; friend, Kimber Anne Engstrom; and gifted editor, Lonnie Hull DuPont.

I want to dedicate this book to my beautiful daughter, Emilie Joy Shepherd, and my precious mother, Carole Goodman.

A special thank-you to all those who stand in the gap for me in prayer, including but not limited to Rhonda, Sue, Anna, Rochelle, Susan, Pam, and Jan.

And to my amazing ministry team of princesses—you are a treasure and a blessing to me. Thank you for who you are and all you do.

INTRODUCTION

We have heard from our King . . . Now it's time to hear from our Prince!

I can't believe it has been five years since I wrote *His Princess: Love Letters from Your King*. Never did I dream that book would be in the hands of over two hundred thousand women and published in three languages. Through the book *His Princess*, we discovered that our Father is the King of Kings and that we truly are royalty, "His Princess."

Now it's time to unveil another treasure of truth—we are also the Bride of Christ, His Princess Bride. If you are ready to enter into a passionate relationship with the Lover of your soul; if you have been wanting your Lord, your Prince, to whisper sacred secrets of eternity to you through His Word . . . then this book was written for you.

May you experience the love of Christ, though it is too great to understand fully. Then you will be made complete with all the fullness of life and power that comes from God.

Ephesians 3:19

My Eternal Bride

I want to reveal a sacred secret to you, My beloved. Although I am your God, I am also your eternal Husband. I will come soon to carry you over the threshold into eternity. My desire is to lift the veil from your eyes that you might see who you really are, My Princess, My Bride. I am the Lover of your soul. I long to get close enough to give you a glimpse of My eternal love for you. If you will seek Me with all your heart, I will reveal Myself to you in extraordinary ways. If you will come before Me and ask, I will give you a new hope in your heart that will change your view of Me, of yourself, and of the world around you forever.

Love,
Your Creator and Husband

The Lord All-Powerful,
the Holy God of Israel,
rules all the earth.
He is your Creator and husband,
and he will rescue you.

ISAIAH 54:5 CEV

My Lord and Husband

I am in awe. What a strange and wondrous thought to think of You, my God, as my eternal Husband. There is something so astonishing about discovering I am Your Bride, the Bride of Christ. Yes, I want You to lift the veil and let me see You as my Prince and me as your Princess Bride. You are the one true love my heart has longed for all my life. So today I stand at Your altar ready to surrender my heart, my soul, and all that I am. . . . May I find myself as I begin to seek You with all that is within me.

Love,
Your Princess Bride

Let us rejoice and be glad
and give him glory!
For the wedding of the Lamb has come,
and his bride has made herself ready.

REVELATION 19:7 NIV

My Beautiful Bride

You are so beautiful to Me. I wish for one moment that you could see what I see when I look at you. When I gaze at you, I see a treasure ready to be discovered, a princess ready to shine, and a bride ready to be loved. When I look at you . . . I love what I see! If you could grasp how beautiful you are in My eyes, then you would never feel insecure again. The beauty I created you to be is a reflection of Me, My love. I created you in My image, so never doubt again that your eternal beauty is a breath of heaven!

Love,
Your adoring Prince

FOR YOUR ROYAL HUSBAND

DELIGHTS IN YOUR BEAUTY;

HONOR HIM, FOR HE IS YOUR LORD.

PSALM 45:11

My Prince

I am ready to let You make me a beautiful reflection of who You are. Let me fix my eyes upon You that I may see myself as You see me. I am ready to walk through the rest of my life as Your Princess Bride. I no longer want anyone but You, my Lord and Prince, to define my true beauty. So please, open my heart that I may receive Your words of truth about who I really am!

Love,

Your Bride
who loves how beautiful You make me feel

I PRAISE YOU BECAUSE I AM
FEARFULLY AND WONDERFULLY MADE;
YOUR WORKS ARE WONDERFUL,
I KNOW THAT FULL WELL.

PSALM 139:14 NIV

You have turned my mourning
into joyful dancing.
You have taken away my clothes of
mourning and clothed me with joy,
that I might sing praises to
you and not be silent.
O LORD my God, I will give
you thanks forever!

PSALM 30:11–12

My Princess Bride

May I invite you to let your heart dance with Me today? Only I can turn your mourning into dancing. I will give you the beauty and grace needed for the world to see that you are My Beautiful Bride. When you dance with Me, you will feel yourself move to the beat of My heart. It is time, My Bride, to put on your dancing shoes. Now allow Me, your Prince, to play a song, a song for your soul. A song that will make your heart beat with Mine now and throughout all eternity.

Love,
Your true Prince Charming

Let them praise his name with dancing
And make music to him with
tambourine and harp.

PSALM 149:3 NIV

My Prince

What an honor, my Lord, I am truly over-
whelmed by Your invitation. How could it
be that I am chosen to dance with the Savior
of the world? Today I place my heart in Your
hands and say yes to Your invitation to dance.
I'm ready to move to the beat of Your heart.
I am ready to step out in faith. I am ready to
dance with You all the days of my life.

Love,

Your Princess
who wants to dance again

My Princess Bride

You have captured My heart, My Princess.
I will always love you. From the moment I
dreamed you up, I loved and adored you. This
love I have for you is never ending and ever
present. My heartfelt desire is for you to walk
through all your days knowing you are truly
the love of My life. I never want you to feel
you have to earn My affection; nothing you
have said or done can or will ever change the
way I feel about you. I have chosen you to be
My precious Bride. If you allow your soul to
settle into Mine and become one with Me,
you will never doubt that I am forever and
always devoted to you.

Love,
Your Prince Jesus
who can't stop loving you

Greater love has no one than this,
that he lay down his life for his friends.

JOHN 15:13 NIV

My Prince

How I long to bathe my soul in your never-ending, ever-cleansing love. Yet, many times I struggle to let You wash away my stains in Your sea of forgiveness. Somehow I feel I don't deserve to be loved, but here I am, ready to cross the threshold and enter into an intimate love relationship with You. Now pour Your living water over me, my Prince, and may I be forever refreshed by You alone.

Love,
Your Princess
who longs to fall in love with You

I love the L‍ORD, for he heard my voice;
he heard my cry for mercy.

....

PSALM 116:1 NIV

THIS IS THE DAY THE LORD HAS MADE;

LET US REJOICE AND BE GLAD IN IT.

....

PSALM 118:24 NIV

My Princess

Come away with Me, My beloved Bride, I
am waiting to show you the world through
My eyes. There's so much for you to see—
don't miss it, My love. Let Me enter into your
world and get close enough to whisper trea-
sures of truth to your spirit. I am here extend-
ing My hand to you. Will you place your hand
in Mine and let your Prince guide your way
today? I want to take you on an extraordinary
adventure with Me. I just want to be close to
My Princess today, to love on you. It's about
us today, so hold on tightly and don't let go.

Love,
Your Lord
who wants to be near you

I LOVE YOUR SANCTUARY, LORD,

THE PLACE WHERE YOUR GLORIOUS

PRESENCE DWELLS.

....

PSALM 26:8

My Prince Jesus

How could I refuse a walk with the Savior of the world? My heart breaks as I reflect on all the days I have missed out on walking closely with You. I imagine You waiting for me each morning, and how it must break Your heart when I forget You are here. Please forgive me for not inviting You to share all my days with me. Today I want to invite You into my day and all my tomorrows. May I never forget to hold Your hand as we stroll through this life together. I love You, Lord.

Love,

Your Bride
who invites You now

My Beautiful Bride

You are never alone, My beloved. When you hurt, I hurt, and it breaks My heart to watch you cry without Me. I am here with you, desiring to be the shoulder your tears fall on. I too walked the world broken, My love. We will work through any and all things together, My Bride. I can and will heal your broken heart. Call out My name, Jesus, in your dark hours, and I will hold you. Will you give Me a chance to love you back to life again? I promise that you will see the light of a new day and joy will come again.

Love,
Your Prince
who will wipe away your tears

He will once again fill your
mouth with laughter
and your lips with shouts of joy.

JOB 8:21

My Prince of Peace

You truly are the love of my life, and Your
Bride is crying out to You now. Yes, come
hold me while I cry. How it comforts my soul
to have access to You anytime. I love knowing I am not alone in the dark. Thank You,
my Prince, my Lord, for reaching down from
heaven with Your loving hand and wiping
away my tears. Hold me until all is well with
my soul again. Remind me when I hurt that
You are just a prayer away.

Love,
Your Bride
who longs to be in Your arms always

But in my distress I cried out to the LORD;
yes, I prayed to my God for help.
He heard me from his sanctuary;
my cry to him reached his ears.

PSALM 18:6

My Precious Bride

I am your hero. I have already died saving your life. I am here to rescue you from drowning in a sea of hopelessness and carry you to shore when you're too weary to swim. I will revive your soul and set your feet back on the solid ground. I will not let anything or anyone keep Me from coming to you when you call. I love to save you from harm, My love, so next time you need to be saved from trouble, call to Me, your Prince, and I will come.

Love,
Your Savior and Rescuer

WHEN YOU PASS THROUGH THE
WATERS, I WILL BE WITH YOU;
AND WHEN YOU PASS THROUGH THE RIVERS,
THEY WILL NOT SWEEP OVER YOU.
WHEN YOU WALK THROUGH THE FIRE,
YOU WILL NOT BE BURNED;
THE FLAMES WILL NOT SET YOU ABLAZE.
....

ISAIAH 43:2 NIV

My Prince Jesus

I am amazed! I have a real hero who saves me! How did I get so blessed that the Savior of the world has become my Prince? How amazing it is to know that You reach down from heaven and save me from drowning in a sea of hopelessness. I really do need You to be my life preserver, Lord. There will never be words to express how much I truly love You.

Love,
Your Princess
who loves to be rescued

HE REACHED DOWN FROM
HEAVEN AND RESCUED ME;
HE DREW ME OUT OF DEEP WATERS.

PSALM 18:16

I will sing to the LORD as long as I live.
I will praise my God to my last breath!
May all my thoughts be pleasing to him,
for I rejoice in the LORD.

PSALM 104:33–34

My Princess Bride

Your life in Me is a symphony. At this moment, you are a song ready to be written by Me, your composer. Your praise is music to My heart, My Bride. I love when you sing to Me, My beloved. If you will let Me, I will put a song in your soul that will be a sweet melody for you to enjoy all the days of your life. Your praise is a blessing to your Prince, and I will bless you for your sacrifice of praise. So open your precious lips, My love, and let Me hear you sing so all of heaven can hear you rejoice!

Love,
Your Prince
who hears from heaven

I will praise you, LORD, with all my heart;
I will tell of all the marvelous
things you have done.
I will be filled with joy because of you.
I will sing praises to your
name, O Most High.

PSALM 9:1–2

My Prince

My heart soars when I enter into praise for You, although somehow, a song of praise seems so simple compared to all You have done for me. But I long to express my deep love to You, my Lord. So if it is my praise that pleases You, I will open my lips and sing my heart out for an audience of one . . . You! And may my life become what my lips cannot say in a song of adoration.

Love,

*Your Princess
who praises You*

My Precious Princess

As My Bride, you can ask Me for anything you need, and I will provide it for you in unexpected ways. I am the one who can meet you in the deepest part of your soul. I am the one who gives you the desires of your heart. I know sometimes you are afraid to believe that I am truly there, but I am. No matter what your life looks like right now, I am working all things together for your good. It is My pleasure to take care of you, so rest in Me, My beloved.

Love,
Your Prince and Provider

And I will do whatever you ask in my name, so that the Son may bring glory to the Father. You may ask me for anything in my name, and I will do it.

My Prince

Please forgive me for all the days I took Your
place in my life by trying to meet my own
needs. Right now, I place my future in Your
loving hands. I am ready to come before Your
throne and trust You, no matter what. Today
I trade all my fears for a renewed faith in You.
Today I know in my heart that You will provide even more than I ask for. . . . May I never
doubt You again!

Love,
Your Princess
who believes in You

And this same God who takes care
of me will supply all your needs
from his glorious riches, which have
been given to us in Christ Jesus.

PHILIPPIANS 4:19

THE LORD IS MY ROCK, MY
FORTRESS, AND MY SAVIOR;
MY GOD IS MY ROCK, IN WHOM
I FIND PROTECTION.
HE IS MY SHIELD, THE POWER THAT SAVES ME,
AND MY PLACE OF SAFETY.
....
PSALM 18:2

My Beloved Bride

The time is now to believe My promises and trust Me to shelter you from the storms that will come in this life. I am truly the knight in shining armor that your heart longs for. I am the one who has already given His life for you. I know your hidden fears, but you must learn to look to Me, My beloved Bride, when life hits hard. I am the rock on which you can stand when all around you seems to be sinking sand. Stand on My Word and hide it in your heart, and you will never sink in hopelessness again!

Love,
Your Prince and Rock

HEAR MY CRY, O GOD;

LISTEN TO MY PRAYER.

FROM THE ENDS OF THE EARTH I CALL TO YOU,

I CALL AS MY HEART GROWS FAINT;

LEAD ME TO THE ROCK THAT IS HIGHER THAN I.

....

PSALM 61:1–2 NIV

My Rescuer

Yes, I need to be saved by You. Please rescue me, my Lord. I need You to be my rock and my strong Prince. I don't want to stand alone anymore. I invite You now to become the strength of my life. Grab hold of my fearful heart and place my feet securely on the rock of Your Word. May I never move from this rock again!

Love,

Your Princess
who is ready to stand

My Cherished Bride

I will never break a promise to you, My Bride. I will always do for you exactly as it is written in My Word. Please don't let those who have disappointed you make you insecure about who I am. Remember, My beloved, I am not man; I am your eternal Husband and your Lord. I am Truth. You never need to worry about whether or not I will come through for you. Every vow I have made to you will prove to be true in My perfect time. Every word I speak is divine truth. I will never disappoint you if you will learn to wait on My perfect time.

Love,
Your Prince
whom you can trust

For your kingdom is an
everlasting kingdom.
You rule throughout all generations.
The LORD always keeps his promises;
he is gracious in all he does.

PSALM 145:13

My Prince

I want to trust You, my Lord, but sometimes I feel like I can't count on anyone to keep his or her word. So please forgive me for doubting You. Help me to remember that You are not like those who have broken their promises to me. You are the one who is faithful and true. Renew my faith from this day forward, and may I never forget all You have already done to prove Your promises are true.

Love,

Your Princess
who is learning to trust

God's way is perfect.
All the LORD's promises prove true.
He is a shield for all who look
to him for protection.

PSALM 18:30

My Treasured Princess

You are so precious to Me, My Princess. There are not enough grains of sand on the earth to express how often I think of you. Day and night I am thinking of you. You are always on My mind. You are hidden in My heart and forever a part of Me. I care about every detail of your life, and I am never too busy to focus on you. So, wherever you are in this big world, take comfort in knowing that My thoughts are with you, My beautiful Bride, and so is My heart.

Love,
Your Prince
who loves thinking of you

HOW PRECIOUS ARE YOUR THOUGHTS
ABOUT ME, O GOD. THEY CANNOT BE
NUMBERED! I CAN'T EVEN COUNT THEM;
THEY OUTNUMBER THE GRAINS OF SAND! AND
WHEN I WAKE UP, YOU ARE STILL WITH ME!

PSALM 139:17–18

My Beloved Prince

I am falling for You more and more every day, my Prince, my Husband. Eternity seems so far away sometimes, yet I know in my heart at any moment I could see You face to face. How I long to feel You close to me. But until that glorious day comes, I must say how wonderful it is to walk through this life knowing the Savior of the world is thinking of me. May I never stop looking for You as You continue to reveal Your love to me each new day.

Love,

Your Bride
who loves knowing I am on Your mind

YOU SAW ME BEFORE I WAS BORN.

EVERY DAY OF MY LIFE

WAS RECORDED IN YOUR BOOK.

EVERY MOMENT WAS LAID OUT

BEFORE A SINGLE DAY HAD PASSED.

....

PSALM 139:16

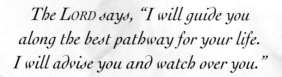

The Lᴏʀᴅ says, "I will guide you
along the best pathway for your life.
I will advise you and watch over you."

PSALM 32:8

My Princess Bride

I am the way, My Bride. Will you allow Me to lead you all the days of your life? Will you let your Prince place your beautiful feet on the path I prepared for you long ago? Come with Me, My love, on a surprising adventure that will thrill your heart. Let Me give you the kind of life that will leave a great legacy. If you will allow Me to lead, I promise you will never be disappointed.

Love,
Your Prince
who longs to guide you

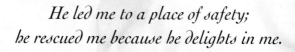

He led me to a place of safety;
he rescued me because he delights in me.

PSALM 18:19

My Prince

Today I say yes to Your leading in my life!
How can I refuse the request of the one who
gave His life for me? I would be honored to
follow You the rest of my time here on earth
until I step with You into Your eternal kingdom. Please take my hand and show me the
way to abundant life, my Lord. Open my ears
that I may hear Your still voice and follow
where You lead.

Love,
Your Princess
who loves the way You lead

My Brave Bride

My courageous Princess, allow Me to fight any and all battles this life brings you. I don't want My Bride to exhaust herself fighting in her own strength. The battle you face, My love, is already won! Now step behind Me and let your powerful Prince shield you from the attacks of the enemy of your soul. Yes, I am your warrior and your protector. As long as you stand behind Me and let Me fight for you, there is nothing that can or will overtake you. It is My pleasure to go to war for My beloved Bride.

Love,
Your Prince and Protector

For the LORD your God is the one who goes with you to fight for you against your enemies to give you victory.

DEUTERONOMY 20:4 NIV

My Prince

I am ready to let You fight for me, my wonderful warrior. I am tired of fighting this battle by myself. You alone are the one who will bring victory to my life. Please forgive me for using my actions and words as weapons to hurt those who have hurt me. Thank You for being my shield and my strength. . . . Thank You for fighting for me. I love You, my Lord!

Love,

Your Princess Bride
who is ready to stand behind You

I love you, LORD;
you are my strength.

································

PSALM 18:1

THE HEAVENS PROCLAIM THE GLORY OF GOD.

THE SKIES DISPLAY HIS CRAFTSMANSHIP.

DAY AFTER DAY THEY CONTINUE TO SPEAK;

NIGHT AFTER NIGHT THEY MAKE HIM KNOWN.

....

PSALM 19:1–2

My Beauty

You can believe in Me, My beloved. It so breaks My heart when you doubt your Prince. What must I do to prove I am who I say I am and that you are Mine? Can I paint you another sunset to kiss you good night? Can I place more stars in the sky to bring a sparkle in your eye? Can I comfort you one more night when you call out to Me? Can I answer another prayer for My Princess? I will do whatever it takes, and I will never stop creating ways to prove to you that I am here.

Love,
Your Prince,
the One who is real

YOUR KINGDOM IS AN EVERLASTING KINGDOM,

AND YOUR DOMINION ENDURES

THROUGH ALL GENERATIONS.

THE LORD IS FAITHFUL TO ALL HIS PROMISES

AND LOVING TOWARD ALL HE HAS MADE.

PSALM 145:13 NIV

My Lord

How many times do I struggle to believe You are truly here with me? Even though You have proved Your presence over and over again, I still allow my heart to doubt. So here I am again, requesting that You will become more real to me than ever before. Please help me, my Prince, that I may never lose my faith in You again. Thank You for Your never-ending patience with Your Princess.

Love,

Your Princess
who believes You now

My Bride

I am the light: "The light of the world." I am your light and the love of your life. When your world feels cold and dark, you can count on Me to warm you from the inside out. You will never stumble and fall if you will allow your Prince to light your way. I see perfectly in the dark, so never fear—I am here to move all the obstacles out of your way, My beloved. And if ever you do stumble in the dark, I will always pick you up with My loving arms. Rest assured, My beauty, there will always be a light on for you to be able to find your way back to Me.

Love,
Your Prince and Illumination

You light a lamp for me.
The LORD, my God, lights
up my darkness.

PSALM 18:28

My Prince

You are the light of my world and the love
of my life. I know that when You are near, I
never need to fear anything or anyone. Please
light my way back to You when I have walked
away. Help me know that not even the darkness can cause me to lose my way. Please hold
me close as I learn to trust Your sight when I
cannot see on my own.

Love,
Your Bride
who will find You

For you are the fountain of life,
the light by which we see.

PSALM 36:9

My Busy Bride

Take a time-out and retreat with Me, My love; I can see your spirit needs a time of refreshing. I am asking you to come away with Me, My beloved Bride. Your eternal Husband wants to give your weary soul replenishment. Leave the cares of this life and let us run away together for a while. Let Me revive your soul as you splash in My rivers full of living water. I am waiting . . . waiting for you . . . whenever you are ready. Come to Me, My love, and we will escape to a peaceful place all alone together.

Love,
Your Prince,
your place of rest

THEN JESUS SAID, "COME TO ME, ALL OF YOU WHO ARE WEARY AND CARRY HEAVY BURDENS, AND I WILL GIVE YOU REST."

....

MATTHEW 11:28

My Prince

I am ready to leave the cares of this life and run away with You. I can't wait to be with You, my Lord. No one refreshes me the way You do. No one soothes my soul and loves me the way You do. Yes, I am ready to leave the world behind and run away with You. Take me now where I may lay beside still waters with You.

Love,
Your Princess,
Yours alone

HE LETS ME REST IN GREEN MEADOWS;

HE LEADS ME BESIDE PEACEFUL STREAMS.

HE RENEWS MY STRENGTH.

HE GUIDES ME ALONG RIGHT PATHS,

BRINGING HONOR TO HIS NAME.

....

PSALM 23:2–3

No one will be able to stand up against
you all the days of your life.
As I was with Moses, so I will be with you;
I will never leave you nor forsake you.

JOSHUA 1:5 NIV

My Beloved Bride

When anyone speaks hurtful words to you, they are coming against Me. You are My vessel of honor and a trophy of My grace. Look to Me for the truth when lies are spoken to you. Anyone who tries to hinder you will have to deal with Me, My love. Hide yourself in My treasured Word, and I will remind you of your immeasurable worth as many times as it takes. I am your Lord and your Prince. The battles you face are not yours, My Bride; they are Mine to fight for you. I can take their insults and attacks, but you are too tender to handle spiritual war all alone. So stand behind Me and let Me defend you until the end!

Love,
Your Lord and Defender

He heals the brokenhearted
and binds up their wounds.

PSALM 147:3 NIV

My Lord

I desperately need You to heal my heart from all the lies that have been spoken to me. Teach me day by day, as I sit with You reading Your Word, what my true identity is. I am ready to trade all the lies for Your truth. I am ready to allow You to renew my mind and refresh my spirit once again. Thank You for never giving up on me even when I give up on myself.

Love,
Your Princess
who loves Your truth

My Princess Bride

I will always come when you call for Me,
My love. Call out to Me as many times as
you need Me, and I will come comfort you. I
never tire of hearing your sweet voice address
My name. When your heart is broken, I
want to put all the pieces back in place for
you. When you feel empty, I will fill you up
again and again. When your spirit has been
crushed, My love, I am here to revive your
soul. Be assured, My Princess, I am always
available to you anytime you need Me. Call to
Me and I will answer.

Love,
Your Prince
who is only a prayer away

The LORD hears his people when
they call to him for help.
He rescues them from all their troubles.
The LORD is close to the brokenhearted;
he rescues those whose spirits are crushed.

PSALM 34:17–18

My Prince

I love to call to You, my Lord. It is an amazing comfort to know that You, the Son of God, hear my cry and come to my rescue. Why am I so blessed to personally know the only one who truly understands what I need to be rescued? Thank You for who You are and all You do for me, my beloved Prince. I am truly blessed to be Your Bride.

Love,
Your Bride
who is forever grateful

*In my distress I called to the L*ORD*;*
I cried to my God for help.
From his temple he heard my voice;
my cry came before him, into his ears.

PSALM 18:6 NIV

HE COVERS THE SKY WITH CLOUDS;

HE SUPPLIES THE EARTH WITH RAIN

AND MAKES GRASS GROW ON THE HILLS.

....

PSALM 147:8 NIV

My Princess Bride

It brings Me great joy to color your world, My beloved Bride. Whenever you begin to doubt My devotion to you, look for Me and I will create new ways to prove to you how passionately I love you. I will paint the sky with a heavenly bliss to uplift your spirit. I will create a radiant rainbow on a cloudy day to remind you that I keep all My promises. I will grow delicate flowers, just to see you smile. I am here to sweeten your days and carry all your burdens for you. I will send a cool breeze to touch your face on a hot day, just to remind you how much I love you.

Love,
Your Lord and Creator

SURELY YOUR GOODNESS AND

UNFAILING LOVE WILL PURSUE ME

ALL THE DAYS OF MY LIFE,

AND I WILL LIVE IN THE HOUSE OF THE LORD

FOREVER.

....

PSALM 23:6

My Prince

Your commitment to me, my Lord, has captivated my heart. I am broken as I reflect on all the days gone by where I did not see the wonderful things on earth that You created for my pleasure. Too many times I've been blinded by the worries of this world. Please, my Prince, open my eyes that I may never miss another day to let You express Your love for me. I do love the way You color my world.

Love,

Your adoring Bride

My Beloved Bride

I know your heart longs to dream. Don't lose sight of your hope, My beloved; I placed that passion inside you to do something great while you are reigning here on earth. I want to be the one to lift you up in My appointed time. If you are willing to wait on Me, I will take you to a place where dreams come true. Let Me be the one who gives you your wings, My Bride. I alone can lift you higher than you could ever fly on your own. You will see the world from a whole new point of view when you soar with Me.

Love,
Your Prince
who lifts you up

But those who trust in the LORD
will find new strength.
They will soar high on wings like eagles.
They will run and not grow weary.
They will walk and not faint.

ISAIAH 40:31

My Prince

You are the wind that takes me where I want to go. You are the sweet incense that makes my life so sweet. Yes, Lord, I will wait on You to give me my wings. Please prepare me for my appointed time to soar. Please be my strength, that I may run this race and never give up or grow weary while waiting. Thank You in advance for my wings.

Love,
Your Bride
who longs to fly with You

Now all glory to God, who is able, through his mighty power at work within us, to accomplish infinitely more than we might ask or think.

EPHESIANS 3:20

My Princess

I know you live in a world where many relationships come to a bitter end, My love. But I am not man; I am your Lord and your Prince. I will never leave you or forsake you, My beloved Bride. As long as you walk with Me, you will never walk alone. I am with you wherever you are, and I will never abandon you. If ever you doubt I am here, just ask Me and I will reveal Myself to you in a very special way. I will do whatever it takes to prove My faithfulness to you. You can trust your heart in My care. I will not let you down as long as you look up.

Love,
Your Prince
who will always be Yours

EVEN WHEN I WALK
THROUGH THE DARKEST VALLEY,
I WILL NOT BE AFRAID,
FOR YOU ARE CLOSE BESIDE ME.
YOUR ROD AND YOUR STAFF
PROTECT AND COMFORT ME.

PSALM 23:4

My Faithful Prince

Thank You for being my one true love. Thank You for being the one who walks in when others walk out of my life. What a comfort to know I am never alone because I am Yours. Your faithfulness is the foundation of my very being. Please, my Lord, open my spiritual eyes that I may see You, that I may feel Your presence and never doubt You are with me.

Love,
Your Princess
who wants to be close

EVEN IF MY FATHER AND MOTHER
ABANDON ME, THE LORD
WILL HOLD ME CLOSE.

....

PSALM 27:10

Surely your goodness and
unfailing love will pursue me
all the days of my life,
and I will live in the house
of the Lord *forever.*

PSALM 23:6

My Bride

It brings Me such great pleasure to watch and see you enjoy the blessings I have arranged for you. I love to surprise My Bride with little gifts that only she can see. Let yourself receive from Me today. Don't let the difficulties of this life cause you to lose sight of who you are and all I have for you. Remember, My love, you are My royalty, you are My treasure. Now look to the heavens and smile because the best is yet to come!

Love,
Your Prince and Blessing

They will tell of the power
of your awesome works,
and I will proclaim your great deeds.
They will celebrate your
abundant goodness
and joyfully sing of your righteousness.

PSALM 145:6–7 NIV

My Generous Prince

I feel like the most blessed Bride to be Yours. I love Your little surprises. Today I open my heart completely to receive all You have for me. I don't want to miss out on anything You have planned for our life together. Please pour out Your favor and blessing upon me. May all the world around me see I am Your Princess. Thank You for the greatest gift of all . . . eternity with You!

Love,
Your Princess
who celebrates all You do

My Bride

There are many things I have to offer you as your eternal Husband. I offer you everlasting life, I give you anytime access to Me. I give you unspeakable joy, an abundant life, and an eternal home. As My Bride, your prayers reach the heavens and people's lives are changed forever because I hear your every word whispered to Me. But there is more, My beloved. I command My angels to stand guard over you. There are many things you have been spared of without you knowing. Just be blessed in knowing I have covered you wherever you have gone, and I will continue to cover you until you are finally home with Me once and for always.

Love,
Your Prince and Sole Provider

Praise the LORD, you angels,
you mighty ones who carry out his plans,
listening for each of his commands.
Yes, praise the LORD, you armies of angels
who serve him and do his will!

PSALM 103:20–21

My Prince

How can I ever say no to receiving the kind of life You offer me? There is no one in the world who can give me the kind of relationship You provide. To be honest, my Lord, when I really think about all You do and all You have done for me, I am almost ashamed about all the times I have taken You for granted. You truly are the Lover of my soul and all I have ever wanted.

Love,

Your Princess
who truly loves you

For he will command his
angels concerning you
to guard you in all your ways.

....

PSALM 91:11 NIV

THE LORD IS MY SHEPHERD;

I HAVE ALL THAT I NEED.

HE LETS ME REST IN GREEN MEADOWS;

HE LEADS ME BESIDE PEACEFUL STREAMS.

HE RENEWS MY STRENGTH.

....

PSALM 23:1–3

I WILL TAKE CARE OF YOU
WHEN YOU'RE SICK

My Princess

I will always be with you in sickness and in health. Let Me, your Lord, comfort you and take you to a place where your soul can be at rest even when your body is ill. I will provide peace and healing for My Princess. You have nothing to fear, My beloved. I was there when you took your first breath, and I will be there when you take your last. I can heal you with just a touch, or I can carry you home to heaven with Me. Just know I will hold you now and until we finally see one another face to face.

Love,
Your Prince and Healer

O LORD MY GOD, I CRIED TO YOU FOR HELP,

AND YOU RESTORED MY HEALTH.

YOU BROUGHT ME UP FROM THE GRAVE, O LORD.

YOU KEPT ME FROM FALLING

INTO THE PIT OF DEATH.

....

PSALM 30:2–3

My Prince

It is so hard on me when I am sick. Please comfort me and touch me with Your healing hands. Give me physical strength when I am weak. I need You to be by my side. I need a touch from my Prince. I am weak but You are my strength. So feed me with spiritual nourishment that I may say, "It is well with my soul."

Love,

*Your Princess
who trusts You*

My Bride

There will be times that you will feel I am far from you. That is not true, My love. Your feelings will deceive you, but I never will. I am the truth that will forever help you find your way back to Me. So whenever you feel lost, just look up, and I will be the one to light your way when you are lost. When your world seems dark, I will be your compass and your comfort. I will carry you over the finish line of your faith when you're too weary to run. You will never be lost as long as you keep your eyes on Me. Even when you don't have the strength to go on, I will become your strength.

Love,
Your Prince and Your Way

You go before me and follow me.
You place your hand of
blessing on my head.
Such knowledge is too wonderful for me,
too great for me to understand!

PSALM 139:5–6

My Wonderful Lord

Thank You from the depths of my soul for continually proving how strong Your passion is for me. Yes, Lord, there are many days I feel lost and very far from You. I know in my heart You never move from me, but somehow no matter how hard I try to stay close to You, I seem to fall away from Your love and truth. I am so in awe that You continue to run after me no matter what I do or say. I am so grateful that You never, ever give up on me.

Love,
Your Princess
who is ready to be found

O LORD, you have examined my heart
and know everything about me.
You know when I sit down or stand up.
You know my thoughts even
when I'm far away.

PSALM 139:1–2

My Princess Bride

I want you to celebrate life with Me. There are so many amazing things we have to look forward to, so don't let this world keep you from celebrating who you are and the wonderful things to come, My beloved. The things that seem sorrowful now will soon be over, but the joys to come will last forever! So stop for a moment. Do something to celebrate the love relationship we have together. Imagine our great and glorious wedding day, and as you do, let your heart bask in the beauty to come.

Love,
Your Prince and Joy

THE SOUNDS OF JOY AND GLADNESS, THE VOICES

OF BRIDE AND BRIDEGROOM, AND THE VOICES

OF THOSE WHO BRING THANK OFFERINGS

TO THE HOUSE OF THE LORD, SAYING,

"GIVE THANKS TO THE LORD ALMIGHTY,

FOR THE LORD IS GOOD;

HIS LOVE ENDURES FOREVER."

JEREMIAH 33:11 NIV

1

My Beloved Prince

Yes, Lord, I will celebrate our love for each other. Thank You for reminding me to celebrate life with You. Who am I, that You would bless me to be Your Princess Bride? I do indeed have much to be thankful for. May my heart never forget to take time to celebrate Your everlasting love for me.

Love,
Your Bride
who loves You

RISE UP, O LORD, IN ALL YOUR POWER.

WITH MUSIC AND SINGING

WE CELEBRATE YOUR MIGHTY ACTS.

PSALM 21:13

But he was pierced for our transgressions,
he was crushed for our iniquities;
the punishment that brought
us peace was upon him,
and by his wounds we are healed.

ISAIAH 53:5 NIV

My Princess Bride

I have covered you with My blood. I loved you with My life. I don't see you the way you see yourself. That is why I paid the ultimate price for any and all things that you have ever done. You are My spotless and pure Bride. Should you refuse to receive My forgiveness, My love, you are saying My death on the cross was not enough for you. When you ask forgiveness, I cast your sin in the sea of forgetfulness and remember it no more. Now dance with the joy of your salvation, My beauty, My Bride . . . because You are free!

Love,
Your Prince and Purity

Oh, what joy for those
whose disobedience is forgiven,
whose sin is put out of sight!
Yes, what joy for those
*whose record the L*ORD *has cleared of guilt,*
whose lives are lived in complete honesty!

PSALM 32:1–2

My Prince

You have given Your life for all my mistakes,
and all You require in return is that I receive
Your gift of a new day and a new life. It is
so hard to believe that all I have ever done
wrong is lost in Your sea of forgetfulness.
How could You love me so immensely that
You would cleanse my guilty stains with Your
blood? Help me truly accept Your life-chang-
ing forgiveness. May I never look back again
at who I was. May I walk the rest of my days
as Your pure Princess Bride.

Love,
Your Bride
who is forever forgiven

My Priceless Bride

It breaks My heart when you doubt what you're worth. I paid the ultimate price to prove to you how valuable you are, My beloved. I have loved you with My life. Whenever you feel insecure about who you are, look to the cross. Nothing you could ever say or do in this life will change the way I feel for you. You are such a treasure to Me. I gave you My life to free you from a worthless life. I came that My Bride would live an abundant life. Walk now in My confidence, not yours . . . and you will begin to feel your true value.

Love,
Your Prince
who values you

For you are a people holy to the LORD
your God. Out of all the peoples on the
face of the earth, the LORD has chosen
you to be his treasured possession.

DEUTERONOMY 14:2 NIV

My Lord

Please forgive Me, My Prince, for not accepting the price You paid for me to become Your Bride. Sometimes I feel so unworthy of being Your Bride. Who am I that you would trade Your life for mine? Who am I that You would take the punishment I deserve and exchange it for what is rightfully Yours in heaven and on earth? To be honest, my Lord, I cannot quite grasp how much You paid for my life. Maybe I never will. One thing I know is I am loved by the Savior of the world, and may that be enough for me to feel like a treasure.

Love,

Your Princess
who values Your love

For where your treasure is,
there your heart will be also.

MATTHEW 6:21 NIV

AND BE SURE OF THIS:

I AM WITH YOU ALWAYS,

EVEN TO THE END OF THE AGE.

....

MATTHEW 28:20

My Beloved Bride

I know sometimes you feel as if there is a veil over your eyes. There are many things you won't understand about this life, but one day I will lift that veil, and you will see that I had a plan and a divine purpose for all you have walked through in this life. One day I will touch your cheek and wipe away the very last tear you will ever cry. One day you will see Me face to face, and heaven and earth will no longer keep us apart. For now, My beloved, I give you My Spirit to guide you every day, and I command My angels to stand guard over you until the day of My return.

Love,
Your eternal Prince

NOW WE SEE BUT A POOR REFLECTION AS IN A
MIRROR; THEN WE SHALL SEE FACE TO FACE.
NOW I KNOW IN PART; THEN I SHALL KNOW
FULLY, EVEN AS I AM FULLY KNOWN.
....
1 CORINTHIANS 13:12 NIV

My Beloved Prince

Please hide me in Your arms of mercy and speak to my spirit, Lord. I need to hear Your still voice once again whisper, "I am here." With all the decay of society I see all around me, I need a glimpse of what is to come. Remind me to be still and let You wash my fears away as I read your written Word. May I live a life driven by eternity and deposit hope into the next generation to come.

Love,

Your Bride
who longs to see Your face

My Beloved

I alone see the secret fears of your heart,
My love. When you are fearful of the storms
that rage in this life, hear Me whisper, "Be
still and know that I am God." Close your
eyes and call out to Me, for I am your Prince
of Peace. I will calm the storm inside your
soul. Every time you allow Me to navigate
your life, you will be reminded that I am your
Captain. You can count on Me. I made the
seas, and I am your lighthouse when you need
hope.

Love,
Your Prince and Savior

He stilled the storm to a whisper;
the waves of the sea were hushed.

PSALM 107:29 NIV

My Prince

Although I know You are always there, I must admit that too many times I have allowed Your truth to be drowned out by the storm I am in. I need You to help me trust You when I feel like I am drowning. May my spirit be so connected to Yours that I hear You whisper, "I am here to save you." I love knowing I have a mighty Savior who can and will save me from any and all storms. Thank You for being my lifesaver.

Love,
Your Princess
who loves being saved by You

For the LORD your God is
living among you.
He is a mighty savior.
He will take delight in you with gladness.
With his love, he will calm all your fears.
He will rejoice over you with joyful songs.

ZEPHANIAH 3:17

My Bride

Let Me settle something in your mind and soul once and for all, My Bride. I don't see you as you see yourself. You see your sin, and I see a forgiven princess. You see who you were, and I see who you will become as I crown you in My glory. You give yourself guilt, and I give you grace. You hold yourself hostage to your past, and I give you the key to freedom in Me. You are lovely in My eyes, and nothing you could say or do will change this truth. Now let Me open your eyes so you may see all I have died for, that you may have a new view of you!

Love,
Your Prince and New Life

"COME NOW, LET'S SETTLE THIS,"
SAYS THE LORD. "THOUGH YOUR SINS
ARE LIKE SCARLET, I WILL MAKE THEM
AS WHITE AS SNOW. THOUGH THEY
ARE RED LIKE CRIMSON, I WILL MAKE
THEM AS WHITE AS WOOL."

ISAIAH 1:18

My Gracious Lord

Thank You, Lord, that You are the Prince of Peace and my place of rest for my restless soul. Yes, You are right, Lord, I struggle to let go of guilt and receive Your grace. I do need You to open my eyes to Your truth. You said on the cross, "It is finished." May I remember the words You spoke as You took Your last breath at Calvary. May I leave the prison of my past forever and place my life in Your hands from this day forward.

Love,

Your Princess
who now sees clearly

THIS GOOD NEWS TELLS US HOW GOD
MAKES US RIGHT IN HIS SIGHT.
THIS IS ACCOMPLISHED FROM
START TO FINISH BY FAITH.
AS THE SCRIPTURES SAY,
"IT IS THROUGH FAITH THAT A
RIGHTEOUS PERSON HAS LIFE."

ROMANS 1:17

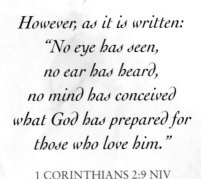

However, as it is written:
"No eye has seen,
no ear has heard,
no mind has conceived
what God has prepared for
those who love him."

1 CORINTHIANS 2:9 NIV

My Beloved Bride

Stop for a moment and close your eyes . . .
dream with Me. Think about that great and
glorious day when we will finally see each
other face to face. Imagine the talks we might
have as we walk along the crystal sea and the
songs we will sing as we celebrate eternity
together. Imagine standing on the streets of
gold I paved for your pretty feet. Be still, My
precious one, and let me renew the eternal
hope in your heart today. Heaven is not just a
dream for you, My beloved. Heaven is reality.

Love,
Your Prince
who loves dreaming about you

And I saw the holy city, the new Jerusalem, coming down from God out of heaven like a bride beautifully dressed for her husband.

REVELATION 21:2

My Prince

When I get discouraged in the days to come,
remind me by Your Holy Spirit to close my
eyes and dream of heavenly things to come.
How my heart longs for the day I am dressed
as Your beautiful Bride. What it will feel like
to finally see you face to face! How awesome
it will be to walk with You in a place with
no more pain. Thank You, my Prince, for
reminding me of what is to come. Yes, I will
dream with You!

Love,
Your Princess
who loves to dream

My Princess Bride

I know how much your heart breaks for the sorrows you sometimes see, My love. Please know that when your heart breaks, so does Mine. It won't always be this way, My beloved Bride. One day I will touch your cheek and wipe away the very last tear you will ever cry. But for now, I want you to pray for those in need of a touch from Me. Hold on to the hope that I will be there soon for My Bride!

Love,
Your Prince and everlasting Joy

He will wipe away every tear from their eyes, and there will be no more death or sorrow or crying or pain. All these things will be gone forever.

REVELATION 21:4

My Prince

My heart does break from what I see, and sometimes I feel helpless. I long to see people free from suffering and pain. Renew the eternal hope in my heart, my Lord. Give me Your unspeakable joy in the midst of the hardships of this life. Give me the passion for people that I need to bring others your gift of everlasting hope and new life. Keep my eyes fixed on the joys to come. Amen!

Love,

Your Princess Bride
who needs You

*The ransomed of the L*ORD *will return.*
They will enter Zion with singing;
everlasting joy will crown their heads.
Gladness and joy will overtake them,
and sorrow and sighing will flee away.

ISAIAH 51:11 NIV

LOOK! I STAND AT THE DOOR AND KNOCK.
IF YOU HEAR MY VOICE AND OPEN THE
DOOR, I WILL COME IN, AND WE WILL
SHARE A MEAL TOGETHER AS FRIENDS.
....
REVELATION 3:20

DINE WITH ME

My Bride

I am knocking at the door of your heart and
hoping you will dine with Me. If you will
open the door, I will come in. I prepared a
feast for you, My beloved. Will you accept My
invitation? I long to feed your hungry soul
until you are completely satisfied. Let your
Prince come in and nourish your spirit, your
mind, and your body. I am the only one who
truly can.

Love,
Your Prince and Satisfaction

YOU PREPARE A TABLE BEFORE ME

IN THE PRESENCE OF MY ENEMIES.

YOU ANOINT MY HEAD WITH OIL;

MY CUP OVERFLOWS.

....

PSALM 23:5 NIV

My Lord

Yes, my Prince, I accept Your invitation to dine. Come feed my hungry soul. Please never stop knocking at the door of my heart, because I desperately need to sit with You each day. I am so honored that You would give me the privilege to dine with You. Please feed my hungry soul, my Lord. There is nothing like Your presence here with me. My cup overflows with Your joy when You satisfy my thirst!

Love,

Your Princess
who is opening the door

My Bride

Call My name in the morning and you will hear Me whisper, "I love you." Seek me and you will feel My presence near you. Whenever you reach for Me, I will extend My hand of mercy to you, My love. My mercies are new every morning for you. Though at times it may feel I am not near you, I am. For you are My love and I will never forsake you. I will keep you warm when the world is cold. You never need to wonder again if I will be there in the morning when you awake.

Love,
Your Prince and Morning Glory

Because of the LORD's great love
we are not consumed,
for his compassions never fail.
They are new every morning;
great is your faithfulness.
I say to myself, "The LORD is my portion;
therefore I will wait for him."

LAMENTATIONS 3:22–24 NIV

Good Morning, My Lord

I love You, my Prince. Will You speak to me in a distinctive way today? I so want to hear Your still voice express Your love for me. I want to be watered with Your Word this morning and walk through this day as the dearly cherished princess You say I am. Although it feels strange to speak to You when I can't see You face to face, I am talking to You in faith and inviting You into my day and all my tomorrows.

Love,

Your Bride
who is ready to be awakened

In the morning, O Lᴏʀᴅ,
you hear my voice;
in the morning I lay my
requests before you
and wait in expectation.

PSALM 5:3 NIV

My Princess

Please don't walk away from Me when life hits hard, My love. I know sometimes you hurt so badly, you want to blame Me. I understand how hard it is for you to keep your heart committed to Me, when you feel I have disappeared in the midst of your despair. I am here and I am working things out for you even when it seems as if nothing has changed. I have My hand on you and extended to you at all times. No one can hold you as close as I can. So don't run from Me, My love. Let Me hold you in My arms of mercy.

Love,
Your Prince and Pursuer

SURELY YOUR GOODNESS AND
UNFAILING LOVE WILL PURSUE ME
ALL THE DAYS OF MY LIFE, AND I WILL LIVE
IN THE HOUSE OF THE LORD FOREVER.

PSALM 23:6

My Prince

Sometimes I want to run away from everything, including You, my Lord. I know I
would be lost without You in my life, so
please don't let me go. I need You to pursue
me every day. I long for You to hold me close
even when my heart is far from You. Let me
experience Your presence day and night.
Thank You for never giving up on me, my
Lord, even when I have given up on myself.

Love,
Your "Runaway" Bride

I LOVE THE LORD BECAUSE HE HEARS MY VOICE

AND MY PRAYER FOR MERCY.

BECAUSE HE BENDS DOWN TO LISTEN,

I WILL PRAY AS LONG AS I HAVE BREATH!

PSALM 116:1–2

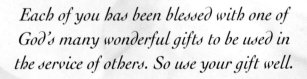

*Each of you has been blessed with one of
God's many wonderful gifts to be used in
the service of others. So use your gift well.*

1 PETER 4:10 CEV

My Gifted Bride

I have placed a gift inside your soul that will bring you great joy and purpose. It's buried inside you, waiting to be discovered. Don't let it be swallowed up by daily distractions and drowned by disappointment. When you are ready to open your heart to Me and receive from your eternal Husband, I will show you how to unwrap your hopes and dreams and teach you to be who I made you to be. I am the giver of every good and perfect gift, so don't be afraid, My beloved, to believe what I say. The gift I offer you is everlasting and priceless.

Love,
Your Gift-giving Prince

*The LORD will fulfill his purpose for me;
your love, O LORD, endures forever —
do not abandon the works of your hands.*

PSALM 138:8 NIV

My Lord and Prince

Here I am, Your Bride, waiting and ready to
let You unwrap the gift You placed inside of
me. I want to use whatever gift You have given
me to further Your kingdom. I love knowing
that my Prince has reached down from heaven
and handed me a present. May I never reject
what You have given, and may I fulfill my des-
tiny as I wait for Your return.

Love,
Your Princess
who wants to be a gift

My Eternal Bride

I have always known you, always loved you, and always been with you. When you were formed, I was with you in your mother's womb. When you took your first breath, I was breathing through you. I know your past and I also know your future. I will walk you through every season of your life, My beloved. I am with you now in spirit. I am the Alpha and the Omega. I am all your new beginnings and your endings. You are part of Me, My love. I am your eternal Husband who will give you your "Happily Ever After." I love you.

Love,
Your Prince
forever and always

"I am the Alpha and the Omega—the beginning and the end," says the Lord God. "I am the one who is, who always was, and who is still to come—the Almighty One."

REVELATION 1:8

My Prince

My mind cannot grasp that You were in all my yesterdays, but my heart soars, knowing that You will be in all my tomorrows. I so look forward to sharing the rest of my life with You, my Prince. I want to laugh with You and cry with You. It brings me immense comfort knowing that You hold my future in the palm of Your hand. I feel like the most blessed bride on earth to be Yours.

Love,

Your Bride
who is in love with You

Look, I am coming soon, bringing my reward with me to repay all people according to their deeds. I am the Alpha and the Omega, the First and the Last, the Beginning and the End.

REVELATION 22:12–13

JESUS REPLIED: "LOVE THE LORD YOUR GOD
WITH ALL *YOUR HEART* AND WITH ALL *YOUR*
SOUL AND WITH ALL *YOUR MIND*. THIS IS THE
FIRST AND GREATEST COMMANDMENT."
....
MATTHEW 22:37–38 NIV

My Princess

Will you surrender all of yourself to Me?
I will never force you to, but I will always
desire that you choose to. Please give Me,
your Husband, a chance to love you the way
I want to. I am the Lover of your soul. Won't
you open your heart and let Me embrace you
with My tender touch? I want to steal your
tender heart from this world and let it flour-
ish in Mine. I want you to get so lost in Me
that nothing can separate us. Come away
with Me, My beloved, and I will complete
you in every way.

Love,
Your Prince
who will wait as long as it takes!

KEEP ME AS THE APPLE OF YOUR EYE;

HIDE ME IN THE SHADOW OF YOUR WINGS.

....

PSALM 17:8 NIV

My Prince

I do love You, Lord. You are the Lover of my soul! How could I not love a prince who loved me with His life? Your love is extravagant and extraordinary in every way. There is none like You. No one can capture my heart the way You do. When I think of eternity with You, I could almost kiss the stars. From this day forward, I give You my heart, my soul, and my mind. I am so ready to immerse myself in Your eternal love for me.

Love,

Your Princess Bride
who is all Yours

My Bride

I came for you to experience a rich life, a life filled with divine purpose, a life like none other. Lose yourself in Me and you will find the true happiness your heart longs for. I am waiting to take you to places that will delight the depths of your soul. Let go of your ways and grab hold of Mine.

Starting now, let Your Prince show you the real way to live. You're Mine, and My Bride must walk blessed by Me. Now take a deep breath and receive the life-giving, soul-satisfying life that is yours for the asking!

Love,
Your Prince and Joy

The thief comes only to steal
and kill and destroy;
I have come that they may have
life, and have it to the full.

JOHN 10:10 NIV

My Prince

My life sometimes feels so meaningless and empty. Show me, my Prince, how to live the kind of life You have for me. I so need Your Holy Spirit to teach me what it means to live as Your Princess Bride. I am ready to leave the old me behind and become like a newly married bride, totally alive from being so in love . . . in love with You, my Lord. Amen!

Love,
Your Princess
who is ready to live!

You will show me the way of life,
granting me the joy of your presence
and the pleasures of living with you forever.

PSALM 16:11

My Princess Bride

I created the heavens and the earth for your
pleasure, My Bride. Yes, the world is yours
to enjoy. Just open your eyes and take a look
around you, My beloved. See what I created
for you to enjoy—the rain to water your soul,
the flowers for you to breathe in and smell
their sweet aroma, the sunsets to kiss you
good night. I gave you mountains to climb.
I placed the stars in the heavens to light
your nights. Yes, My Bride, this is for you.
Take this moment and breathe in the blessed
beauty I created for your pleasure,
My Princess.

Love,
Your Prince
who created this day for you

MAY THE LORD RICHLY BLESS
BOTH YOU AND YOUR CHILDREN.
MAY YOU BE BLESSED BY THE THE LORD,
WHO MADE HEAVEN AND EARTH.

....

PSALM 115:14–15

My Beloved Lord

It saddens me as I reflect on all the sunsets
You painted for me that I have missed. For
the flowers I forgot to smell and the wind
that whispered You loved me. Please forgive
me, my Lord, for getting so caught up in
my world that I have forgotten to enter into
Yours. Yes, I will walk with You today, and
may I never forget to appreciate another
expression of Your love for me!

Love,

Your Princess
who will look for You

THE HEAVENS ARE YOURS, AND
THE EARTH IS YOURS,
EVERYTHING IN THE WORLD IS
YOURS—YOU CREATED IT ALL.

PSALM 89:11

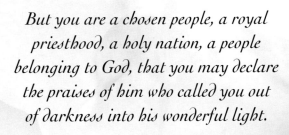

But you are a chosen people, a royal priesthood, a holy nation, a people belonging to God, that you may declare the praises of him who called you out of darkness into his wonderful light.

1 PETER 2:9 NIV

My Bride

I know there are many times you don't feel
like you are royalty, My beloved, but you are.
How you feel does not define who you are.
You are My treasure and the love of My life.
Every day your feelings may change, but Mine
never will. Nothing can take away your royal
position, for it is sealed by My blood. Now
walk in your true identity and never doubt
again that you are My chosen to reign for
such a time as this, as My Princess Bride.

Love,
Your Prince
who chose You

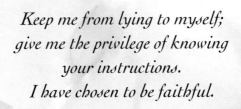

Keep me from lying to myself;
give me the privilege of knowing
your instructions.
I have chosen to be faithful.

PSALM 119:29–30

My Prince

Lord, I need You to help me trade the lies I believe about myself for the truth of who You say I am, "Your Princess Bride." As much as I want to believe this about myself, many layers of lies must be peeled away. You alone are the only one who can give me a renewed mind. So here I stand in light of Your truth and ask for a sweet release by a touch from You.

Love,
Your Bride
who longs to believe

My Princess

I am here, My beloved. Now let Me carry your burdens for you. My shoulders are strong enough to hold all that is too heavy for you to carry on your own. I am your eternal Husband; I am in your life to lighten your load. Now tell your Prince what I need to take from you that you may pursue your life in peace. Whatever it is, My love, I can take it. Please open your hand and place your cares on Me. I want to give you some rest for your weary soul and see you smile again!

Love,
Your strong Prince

Come to me, all you who are weary and burdened, and I will give you rest.

MATTHEW 11:28 NIV

My Prince of Peace

My spirit is weak from this load I have tried to carry alone. How I need You to take my burdens from me, my Lord. I have held them so long I feel like I am stuck under a pile of problems. Please come to my rescue and take this heavy load from Your Bride. What a blessing to know that You are so strong and mighty when I am weak. No one knows how to lighten my life better than You, my Prince!

Love,

*Your tired Princess
who is ready to rest*

Take my yoke upon you and learn from me, for I am gentle and humble in heart, and you will find rest for your souls. For my yoke is easy and my burden is light.

MATTHEW 11:29-30 NIV

PLACE ME LIKE A SEAL OVER YOUR HEART,

LIKE A SEAL ON YOUR ARM;

FOR LOVE IS AS STRONG AS DEATH,

ITS JEALOUSY AS ENDURING AS THE GRAVE.

LOVE FLASHES LIKE FIRE,

THE BRIGHTEST KIND OF FLAME.

MANY WATERS CANNOT QUENCH LOVE,

NOR CAN RIVERS DROWN IT.

IF A MAN TRIED TO BUY LOVE

WITH ALL HIS WEALTH,

HIS OFFER WOULD BE UTTERLY SCORNED.

SONG OF SOLOMON 8:6–7

My Bride

I am truly the Lover of your soul. Won't you allow yourself to become one with your Lord, My beloved? I will wait until you are ready to let your life become hidden in Me. If you will allow My intense love to settle into your soul, we will become like a beautiful dance, a single melody filled with heavenly harmony. Will you let Me close enough to become one song, one flesh, intertwined together for all eternity? I am here waiting to love you like you have never been loved before.

Love,
Your Prince
who loves being one with You

MAKE VOWS TO THE LORD YOUR
GOD, AND KEEP THEM.
LET EVERYONE BRING TRIBUTE
TO THE AWESOME ONE.
....
PSALM 76:11

My Prince

Yes! I want to become one with You now and forever, my Lord. I yield my heart to Yours and enter into this everlasting covenant that You speak of. For where You lead, I will go, and where You stay, I will stay. Your ways will become my ways. I long to become one with You from this day forward. You will forever and always be my God and my eternal Husband. How blessed am I to be Your Bride!

Love,

Your Bride
who is lost in You

My Princess Bride

I am preparing your dream home in heaven right now as you read this letter. I can hardly wait to see your face when I carry you over the threshold and place you, My beautiful Bride, in your eternal dwelling place. This place your Prince is preparing for you is beyond anything you could imagine on your own. When you are finally home with Me, we will walk together by the crystal sea on streets paved more beautifully than the finest of gold. Angels will sing all around us as we celebrate life together forever.

Love,
Your eternal Architect

However, as it is written:
"No eye has seen,
no ear has heard,
no mind has conceived
what God has prepared for
those who love him."

1 CORINTHIANS 2:9 NIV

My Prince

It already feels like home when I enter into Your presence, my Prince. I too long for the day You will carry me home. I imagine the sound of the angels rejoicing. What my heart will feel when I am in my forever place that You personally prepared for me! I love meditating on the miraculous things I have to look forward to as Your Bride. May I keep my eyes fixed on eternity so the things of earth will never again steal my joy of living for You.

Love,
Your eternal Bride
who longs to be home

Then I saw a new heaven and a new earth, for the old heaven and the old earth had disappeared. And the sea was also gone. And I saw the holy city, the new Jerusalem, coming down from God out of heaven like a bride beautifully dressed for her husband.

REVELATION 21:1–3

My Princess Bride

The time is now, My beloved Bride, to get ready for My return. I will come quickly for you, and in that moment you will be changed. I want you to live as if there were no tomorrow. I want your heart and mind fixed on eternity with Me. If you will do as I request, you will be ready for Me when I come. I promise you this, Princess; nothing here on earth is everlasting but My love for you. Now let Me dress you in humility and clothe you in righteousness until I walk you down the aisle of eternity.

Love,
Your eternal Husband

LET US REJOICE AND BE GLAD

AND GIVE HIM GLORY!

FOR THE WEDDING OF THE LAMB HAS COME,

AND HIS BRIDE HAS

MADE HERSELF READY.

···

REVELATION 19:7 NIV

My God, My Groom

Today I say, "I do" and "I will." Get ready for our royal wedding day. I take You, my eternal Husband, loving what I know of You and trusting what I do not yet know.

For better or for worse,
   for richer or for poorer,
   in times of sickness and in times of health,
   in times of joy and in times of sorrow,
   in times of failure and in times of triumph,
   in times of plenty and in times of want,
   to have and to hold from this day forward
   until death places me in Your arms.

Love,
Your Princess Bride
who says "I DO"

I SAW THE HOLY CITY, THE NEW JERUSALEM,
COMING DOWN OUT OF HEAVEN FROM GOD,
PREPARED AS A BRIDE BEAUTIFULLY DRESSED
FOR HER HUSBAND. AND I HEARD A LOUD
VOICE FROM THE THRONE SAYING, "NOW THE
DWELLING OF GOD IS WITH MEN, AND HE WILL
LIVE WITH THEM. THEY WILL BE HIS PEOPLE,
AND GOD HIMSELF WILL BE WITH THEM AND BE
THEIR GOD. HE WILL WIPE EVERY TEAR FROM
THEIR EYES. THERE WILL BE NO MORE DEATH
OR MOURNING OR CRYING OR PAIN, FOR THE
OLD ORDER OF THINGS HAS PASSED AWAY."
HE WHO WAS SEATED ON THE THRONE SAID,
"I AM MAKING EVERYTHING NEW!" THEN
HE SAID, "WRITE THIS DOWN, FOR THESE
WORDS ARE TRUSTWORTHY AND TRUE."

REVELATION 21:2–5 NIV

CLOSING THOUGHTS
FROM THE AUTHOR

I pray that as you have read through these love letters you have discovered that God's love, power, and promises are for you. But I could not let you close this book without making sure you know the King personally—because reading about God's love is not enough to secure a place in His eternal kingdom. We need to accept His invitation and receive the gift of His Son Jesus Christ. I would love the privilege of being a part of your eternal crowning by asking you to say this simple prayer with me:

> Dear God, I don't want to live without You any longer. I believe You sent Your Son to die for me, and I want Him to be my Lord

and my King. I confess my sin and my need for a Savior, and I accept Your free gift of everlasting life. I thank You for writing my name in Your book of life. I pray this prayer by faith in Jesus' name. Amen

If this is your sincere prayer, you can know that angels are rejoicing and the Holy Spirit of the living God is now in you. If I don't have the honor of meeting you during your reign through this life, I look forward to celebrating with you on the other side of eternity. Until then, may our King bless your walk with Him.

Love,
Your sister in Christ,
Sheri Rose

The Spirit and the bride say, "Come." Let anyone who hears this say, "Come." Let anyone who is thirsty come. Let anyone who desires drink freely from the water of life.

Revelation 22:17

Sheri Rose Shepherd is the bestselling author of *His Princess: Love Letters from Your King* and several other books. She has overcome a life of challenges, including a broken childhood home, dyslexia, and weight problems, to bring women around the world the message that God loves them dearly. Shepherd speaks to tens of thousands of women every year. Her story has been one of the most popular shows on *Focus on the Family*. She was recently featured on the *Billy Graham Primetime Television Special*, seen nationwide.

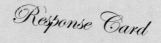

Response Card

I would to love hear from you!

If you'd like to know more about my ministry, the His Princess Bible study on DVD, and the His Princess conference tour, visit our website at www.HisPrincess.com or call 602-407-8789.

His Princess®
M I N I S T R I E S

You're **invited** to hear the message that
has *inspired* more than 500,000 *women* . . .

#1 Show of the Year,
Focus on the Family Radio

Featured on *Billy Graham*
National Primetime TV Special

Bestselling author/speaker
Sheri Rose Shepherd

* Women's Conferences
* Six-Week Bible Studies
* Weekend Retreats on DVD

Sheri Rose's Story

Sheri Rose at age 16 . . . and today.

Sheri Rose Shepherd can relate to almost any woman's battle. She was raised in a dysfunctional home and battled depression, drug abuse, an eating disorder, and a food addiction that left her more than 60 pounds overweight.

In spite of a learning disorder—dyslexia—and her high school English teacher telling her she was "born to lose," Sheri Rose, in God's strength, has become a bestselling author and motivational speaker.

She is the founder of His Princess Ministries, and her book *His Princess: Love Letters from Your King* has spent many weeks on the international bestseller list and has sold more than 250,000 copies in four languages.

Her humorous, heartwarming stories mixed with truth and transparency renew our faith by reminding us how much we are truly loved and adored by our Father in heaven. Once you hear Sheri Rose speak, you will never again doubt that you are . . . *God's Chosen Princess*.

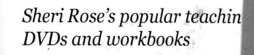